# Sudden Selector's Guide
## to Government Publications

# ALCTS/CMS SUDDEN SELECTOR'S SERIES

# SUDDEN SELECTOR'S GUIDE

## to Government Publications

ALEXANDRA SIMONS

Mary Feeney
*Volume Editor*

Collection Management Section of the Association
for Library Collections & Technical Services
*a division of the American Library Association*
CHICAGO   2017

While extensive effort has gone into ensuring the reliability of information appearing in this book, the publisher makes no warranty, express or implied, on the accuracy or reliability of the information, and does not assume and hereby disclaims any liability to any person for any loss or damage caused by errors or omissions in this publication.

The paper used in this publication meets the minimum requirements of American National Standard for Information Sciences—Permanence of Paper for Printed Library Materials, ANSI Z39.48-1992.

ISBNs
978-0-8389-8915-9 (print)
978-0-8389-8916-6 (PDF)

**Library of Congress Cataloging-in-Publication Data**
Names: Simons, Alexandra, author.
Title: Sudden selector's guide to government publications / Alexandra Simons; Mary Feeney, volume editor.
Description: Chicago : Collection Management Section of the Association for Library Collections & Technical Services, a division of the American Library Association, 2017. | Includes bibliographical references and index.
Identifiers: LCCN 2017004126 | ISBN 9780838989159 (print) | ISBN 9780838989166 (pdf)
Subjects: LCSH: Acquisition of government publications–United States. | Documents libraries—Collection development--United States. | Depository libraries—United States. | Libraries–United States–Special collections–Government publications. | Documents librarians–United States. | Federal Depository Library Program. | United States. Government Publishing Office.
Classification: LCC Z688.G6 S523 2017 | DDC 025.17/34–dc23 LC record available at https://lccn.loc.gov/2017004126

Printed in the United States of America

21 20 19 18 17    5 4 3 2 1

# CONTENTS

## Chapter 5

# FOREWORD

Is subject-area knowledge for collection development still necessary or even important in these days of tightening budgets, vendor selection, and nearly-instant access? My answer is a resounding "Yes!" It is vital for selectors to have an understanding of how their subjects "work," in terms of research, publication, and selection; selectors link a library's collection to its local audience, meeting the needs of researchers and faculty as well as the broader community. Selection by vendors, in the form of approval plans, can indeed create workflow efficiencies, but it takes a knowledgeable selector to set up an effective plan that can account for local needs as well as budgetary and space restrictions. The time saved by such plans allows selectors to both hone the margins of a collection to strengthen it and to conduct increasingly valuable liaison work with user groups. The ongoing purpose of the *Sudden Selector's Guide* series is to provide current information on selection in specific subject areas and to assist selectors in creating a manageable process in unfamiliar subject territories.

Helene Williams
Editor, *Sudden Selector's Guide* Series
September 2016

# PREFACE

## On the Sudden Selector's Series

The *Sudden Selector's Guide* series was created by the Collection Management Section (formerly Collection Management & Development Section) of the Association for Library Collections & Technical Services division of the American Library Association. It is designed to help library workers become acquainted with the tools, resources, individuals, and organizations that can assist in developing collections in new or unfamiliar subject areas. These guides are not intended to provide a general introduction to collection development but to quickly furnish tools for successful selection in a particular subject area. However, there are many tools that are pertinent for all subject areas and although not explored in detail in the guides, the following should be mentioned.

### GUIDES TO COLLECTION DEVELOPMENT

Evans, G. Edward, and Margaret Zarnosky Saponaro. *Collection Management Basics*, 6th ed. Westport, CT: Libraries Unlimited, 2012.

This text serves as an authority on all areas of collection development, from user assessment, collection development policies, evaluation, deselection, and legal issues. This popular resource, in its many editions, has served as a standard text in collection development training.

Johnson, Peggy. *Fundamentals of Collection Development and Management*, 3rd ed. Chicago, IL: American Library Association, 2014.

This guide by one of the key authorities in collection development covers many of the same areas as Evans and Edward. Johnson provides a comprehensive overview of the issues such as policies, planning, developing and managing collections, marketing and outreach activities, and collection analysis. The writing is engaging and its information is useful for both beginning professionals and seasoned selectors.

Disher, Wayne. *Crash Course in Collection Development*. Westport, CT: Libraries Unlimited, 2007.

This title is part of the Crash Course series from Libraries Unlimited, and is aimed toward a new selector without any selection experience or for those with little to no professional experience. Although the general concepts covered may be useful for academic librarians just starting out, it is focused toward the needs of public librarians.

Gorman, G. E., and Ruth H. Miller. *Collection Management for the 21st Century: A Handbook for Librarians*. Westport, CT: Libraries Unlimited, 1997.

Although a bit older than the other texts in this list, the essays address many crucial issues and challenges still of critical concern in collection development. The handbook provides a thorough review of the trends and emerging issues in the field.

Burgett, James, John Haar, and Linda L. Phillips. *Collaborative Collection Development: A Practical Guide for Your Library*. Chicago, IL: American Library Association, 2004.

This guide provides first-hand experience and advice for successful collaborative collection building. The guide provides models and strategies for research, budgeting, promotion, and evaluation.

Alabaster, Carol. *Developing an Outstanding Core Collection: A Guide for Libraries*. Chicago, IL: American Library Association, 2002.

This handbook provides instructions on how to build an adult public library collection from the ground up as well as the tools to maintain an existing collection. The guide provides a wealth of resources for public library collection development as well as sample core lists.

## REVIEW SOURCES

### Choice
www.ala.org/acrl/choice

Reviews in *Choice* magazine, published monthly by the American Library Association, and *Choice Reviews Online* are targeted to academic library collections and emphasize the importance of the title in collection development and scholarly research. *Choice* includes approximately 600 reviews (per month) organized by sub-discipline for books, electronic media and internet resources, as well as publisher advertisements and announcements for new and forthcoming publications. *Choice Reviews Online* provides access to issues from 1998 to the present. There are added features to the online version of the magazine including personalized profiles and title lists and an advanced search screen.

### Library Journal Book Reviews
http://reviews.libraryjournal.com

### Library Journal Prepub Alert
http://reviews.libraryjournal.com/category/prepub

*Library Journal* magazine provides brief reviews of titles on all topics and is aimed for both public and academic libraries. The reviews provide a brief summary of the title and recommendations for library audience and selection. Reviews are available in print issues of the magazine and online through various databases and as a weekly email for new review title alerts.

### Booklist
www.ala.org/offices/publishing/booklist
www.booklistonline.com

*Booklist*, a publication of the American Library Association, publishes more than 8,000 recommended-only reviews of books, audio books, reference sources, video, and DVD titles each year. *Booklist* also provides coverage of ALA award-winning titles and is available online with enhanced content such as advanced searching options and personalized profiles and lists.

*Publisher's Weekly*
www.publishersweekly.com

This magazine is also available through an online subscription and serves as a trade publication for professionals in the library and publishing fields. Its coverage includes industry news, trends, events and book reviews. More than 7,000 book reviews are published annually and written by both freelance reviewers as well as well-known authors. The reviews are divided by fiction and non-fiction.

## ELECTRONIC DISCUSSION LISTS AND WEBSITES

### COLLDV-L

http://serials.infomotions.com/colldv-l

COLLDV-L includes issues of acquisition but also covers more broad issues of collection management, such as policy development, deselection issues, and collection evaluation. It is a moderated discussion directed towards library collection development professionals, bibliographers, selectors, and others involved with library collection development.

### ERIL-L

www.eril-l.org

ERIL-L's purpose is to cover all aspects of electronic resources in libraries. In addition to collection management librarians, participants include reference personnel, systems librarians, and vendors with topics ranging from usage statistics to product issues to licensing. The list is moderated and archived.

### Association for Library Collections & Technical Services (ALCTS) Collection Management Section (CMS)

www.ala.org/alcts/mgrps/cms

The purpose of CMS is to contribute to library service and librarianship through encouragement, promotion of, and responsibility for those activities of ALCTS relating to collection management and development, selection, and evaluation of library materials in all types of institutions. The section develops publications, online courses, and other tools for the training and further development of collection management.

This list is not meant to be exhaustive, but simply an introduction to some of the resources available for getting up to speed in collection development. As the *Sudden Selector* guides are subject-specific, most of the above resources are too general for inclusion in the main text. However, personnel responsible for collection development should ultimately be familiar with most of them. Additionally, for the most exhaustive bibliographies for further research, consult the guides to collection development listed above.

*Doug Litts*
Smithsonian Institution Libraries
American Art Museum & National Portrait Gallery
Editor, *Sudden Selector's Guide* Series 2006–2009

*Helene Williams*
Editor, *Sudden Selector's Guide* Series, 2009–2017
Updated 2016

# INTRODUCTION AND OVERVIEW

*Once you become a 'documents person'. . . you*
*are one for life, even if you move on to other*
*niches or jobs.* (Ennis, 2007)

Welcome to the world of government information! This guide is based on my own experiences as a beginning government information librarian. Having now been the coordinator of my library's government information collection for several years, I feel confident that the resources and information in this guide will help you become a well-rounded, informed, and enthusiastic government information professional.

Learning any new subject area takes time, especially in an area as complex as government information. Although I took a very good government documents course while working on my library science degree, I did not have much experience with government resources and was not really clear on how they were managed and classified and what they contained. However, as with any new experience, I learned more the longer I worked with the collection and interacted with other government information librarians. Government resources contain a breadth of information, and they are valuable resources for academic and general research inside and outside an academic library setting. It is gratifying to introduce users to resources of which they had been completely unaware, especially when most of these resources are usually free and easily accessible.

## THE PURPOSE AND FOCUS OF THIS GUIDE

The purpose of this guide is to help you understand how to manage, coordinate, and market your library's government information collection. It is aimed primarily at librarians new to working as part of the Federal Depository Library Program (FDLP), either for a repository, which receives one hundred percent of government documents distributed by the Government Printing Office (GPO), or for a selective, which receives selected government publications based on particular areas of interest. However, it can also be used by librarians who need an overview of government and related resources. With so many options available online, knowing about government resources is very helpful in most subject areas and for general patron requests. Most likely you will also deal with local, state, and international government and government-related resources, so resources are included here to help you understand and manage them accordingly.

## COLLECTION RESOURCES
## FOR GOVERNMENT INFORMATION

Most of the guides in the *Sudden Selector's* series focus on one specific academic subject and include general collection aids used by selectors such as journals, guides, and university publishers. They also identify vendors that deal specifically with that subject area. These kinds of resources have not typically been used by government information librarians because the majority of tangible and electronic items in US Federal Government collections have come directly from the GPO. These items have then been distributed to participating libraries directly through the FDLP. However, for the past several years many government documents, reports, and other information have been uploaded directly to agency websites, bypassing the GPO completely. Unlike officially cataloged GPO documents, these resources can disappear at any time, or may not be findable by users who really need them. There are also websites and databases containing valuable government-related information outside of the GPO's jurisdiction. I have tried to include many of these agency and related sites in this guide.

The chapters in this guide are:

Chapter 1: Getting Up to Speed

Chapter 2: The Federal Depository Library Program (FDLP)
Chapter 3: Managing the Collection
Chapter 4: US Government and Related Sources
Chapter 5: Issues, Challenges, and Opportunities

In brief, this guide covers the basics of US Federal Government documents, including the history and role of the GPO and the FDLP; how to assess and manage the tangible (print, microfiche, CD-ROM) and electronic resources in your collection; how to find agencies and data outside the FDLP; and how to stay current on the issues, challenges, and opportunities facing the FDLP, GPO, and government information librarians today. You will also find resources and ideas to help you market your collection physically and virtually. Also included are ways to incorporate government information into classroom instruction for undergraduate and graduate research.

This guide does not contain long lists of government publications, go into the minutia of cataloging, or deeply annotate all the various local, state, federal, and international agencies. That would entail a lot more than the number of pages allotted for this guide. However, I have included citations to books and online resources to help you learn more about these areas.

While it is certainly true that many documents librarians learn about government publications through self-instruction and trial and error, please remember that you are not in this alone. You will quickly find that government information librarians make up one of the most responsive, friendly, and informative communities around. I highly recommend that you become involved in your national or state library association's government information groups, such as the American Library Association's (ALA) Government Documents Round Table (GODORT) or the Map and Geospatial Information Round Table (MAGIRT). Many large urban areas often have government information groups with members from public, law, academic, and special libraries, so check to see if there is one in your area. Periodic meetings with these local groups are especially good for comparing notes on collection management, development, outreach, and the current status of government information in general. For those of you in smaller areas, you can keep in touch with other federal depository libraries (FDLs) on the state and regional level and through the FDLP Desktop site.

As with most printed guides, some websites and proprietary databases may have changed names or URLs, or disappeared altogether by the time this book is published. There are now multiple places to find copies of digitized government documents, from proprietary databases to free online websites. The quality of metadata and search capabilities varies greatly from site to site, but I have tried to include the most useful databases and websites that I access on a regular basis and those that are recommended by other librarians.

## ACCESS TO GOVERNMENT INFORMATION AND KNOWING YOUR USERS

While the main focus of this guide is on collection management in an academic library, it is also important to understand the research needs of students, faculty, staff, and the surrounding community for government information. Many government agencies have user-friendly websites containing a wealth of information, but many people do not know about them. Part of your job is to promote these resources to your users (e.g., highlighting the IRS.gov site at tax time). In my experience, most academic libraries' documents collections usually do not get much foot traffic from students or faculty or from the general public. Most queries come in via email and phone and can usually be handled online. To see if there are any patterns to user queries, keep a log of requests for government information for a few months. For frequently asked questions, you may want to set up a general online guide (using Springshare's LibGuides or similar guide software) or a blog that includes relevant local, state, and US government sites. This can also be helpful for reference desk personnel when you are not available. Make sure to update the information periodically. If you have a discovery platform, work with your web services personnel to make government resources easily findable.

If users need very detailed information that you cannot provide right away, let them know that you are working on the issue. I often post queries to state and national FDLP and GODORT online community discussion groups. Government information librarians usually respond very quickly, and someone is sure to have an answer or can point you in the right direction. Libraries no longer part of the FDLP can still access the FDLP's online site. Also, contact your state library or repositories for help and guidance.

## CITING GOVERNMENT DOCUMENTS

Citation of government resources can be tricky, and for researchers and legal scholars, correct citation is vital. The American Psychological Association (APA) and Modern Language Association (MLA) have specific citation guidelines in their print and online guides. I also highly recommend the following:

> *The Bluebook: A Uniform System of Citation*, published by the Harvard Law Review Association. This reference guide is primarily used in legal work, both American and foreign.

*Citing Government Documents,* www.unk.edu/academics/library
.aspx?id=8930, an online guide from the University of Nebraska
Kearney.

*Cite Right,* from the University of Chicago Press. Citations include
those used in the sciences and other disciplines.

## References

Ennis, Lisa A. 2007. *Government Documents Librarianship: A Guide to the Neo-
depository Era.* Medford, NJ: Information Today, Inc.

## Recommended Reading

Cheverie, Joan F., ed. 1998. *Government Information Collections in the Networked
Environment: New issues and Models.* Binghamton, NY: The Haworth Press.

Federal Depository Library Program. 2011. *Legal Requirements & Program Regulations
of the Federal Depository Library Program.* Washington, DC: US Government
Printing Office.

GODORT Education Committee. 2009. *U.S. Federal Government Information
Competencies for Beginning Government Information and General Reference
Librarians.* http://wikis.ala.org/godort/images/a/af/Federal_gov_competencies.pdf.

Forte, Eric J., Cassandra J. Hartnett, and Andrea Sevetson. 2016. *Fundamentals of
Government Information: Mining, Finding, Evaluating, and Using Government
Resources,* 2nd ed. New York, NY: Neal-Schuman Publishers, Inc.

Harvard Law Review Association. 2010. *The Bluebook: A Uniform System of Citation,*
19th ed. Cambridge, MA: Harvard Law Review Association.

Hernon, Peter, and Charles R. McClure. 1988. *Public Access to Government
Information: Issues, Trends, and Strategies,* 2nd ed. Norwood, NJ: Ablex Publishing
Corporation.

Hernon, Peter, Charles R. McClure, and Gary R. Purcell. 1985. *GPO's Depository
Library Program: A Descriptive Analysis.* Norwood, NJ: Ablex Publishing Corporation.

Hernon, Peter, Harold C. Relyea, Robert E. Dugan, and Joan F. Cheverie. 2002.
*United States Government Information: Policies and Sources.* Westport, CT: Libraries
Unlimited.

Kumar, Suhasini L., ed. 2006. *The Changing Face of Government Information: Providing
Access in the Twenty-First Century.* Binghamton, NY: Haworth Information Press.

Lipson, Charles. 2006. *Cite Right: A Quick Guide to Citation Styles—MLA, APA,
Chicago, the Sciences, and More.* Chicago, IL: University of Chicago Press.

Morehead, Joe. 1999. *Introduction to United States Government Information,* 6th ed.
Englewood, CO: Libraries Unlimited, Inc.

Morrison, Andrea M., ed. 2008. *Managing Electronic Government Information in
Libraries: Issues and Practices.* Chicago, IL: American Library Association.

Morrison, Andrea M., and Barbara J. Mann. 2004. *International Government
Information and Country Information: A Subject Guide.* Westport, CT: Greenwood
Press.

# one

# Getting Up to Speed

Included in this chapter are guides, journals, and other resources to help you learn how federal US government information is managed and collected in both print and electronic formats. Also featured are resources that cover government-related topics.

## GUIDES

I highly recommend and often consult the following guides. If your library does not have them and cannot get them for the collection, I suggest that you purchase them for your personal library (Amazon or its resellers usually have them at very reasonable prices). As with any print resource, some of the websites listed in these guides may no longer be available or the URLs may have changed.

Ennis, Lisa A. 2007. *Government Documents Librarianship: A Guide to the Neo-depositing Era*. Medford, NJ: Information Today, Inc.

This guide is especially useful for new depository librarians learning how to manage tangible and digital resources. Ennis covers all aspects of collection management, with the focus on electronic resources, and also suggests ways to market government information collections. Chapter 8, dealing with technical services issues such as cataloging and bibliographic control, processing, and preservation of tangible items, is particularly helpful for librarians whose duties do not include cataloging or processing. The book also contains several very helpful appendices that include additional resources, a self-study template, and a sample of the FDLP's Biennial Survey.

Forte, Eric J., Cassandra J. Hartnett, and Andrea Sevetson. 2016. *Fundamentals of Government Information: Mining, Finding, Evaluating, and Using Government Resources,* 2nd ed. New York, NY: Neal-Schuman Publishers, Inc.

Now in its second edition, this is an essential guide for understanding the different kinds of information available through various government departments and agencies. Chapter titles include "How to think Like a Government Documents Librarian," "Congressional Publications," "The Executive Branch," "Statistical Information," and "Regulations." There are also chapters covering resources on health information, scientific and technical information, the environment, and other areas of research.

Herman, Edward, and Theodora Belniak. 2016. *Locating U.S. Government Information Handbook,* 3rd ed. Buffalo, NY: William S. Hein & Co., Inc.

This is an excellent handbook for finding information from the three branches of the federal government, and the latest edition is intended especially to be used in conjunction with the numerous online resources listed in each chapter. These resources range from government sites (.gov), general websites, proprietary databases (accessed from law or other libraries), and places to find televised hearings and films from the government, such as FedFlix (available through the InternetArchive), YouTube, and C-SPAN. There are excellent and detailed screenshots provided in each chapter to help researchers conduct their own searches. As with many printed guides, links can often become obsolete but these screenshots give the user a good basic structure to follow.

Hernon, Peter, Harold C. Relyea, Robert E. Dugan, and Joan F. Cheverie. 2002. *United States Government Information: Policies and Sources.* Westport, CT: Libraries Unlimited.

This was my textbook in library school, and I still refer back to it often to find information on agencies and policies that apply to government

information access. Topics include government information management issues, handling Freedom of Information Act (FOIA) requests,
national security, trademarks and patents, statistics, core US federal government agencies, the FDLP, historic and present-day resources, and a
wealth of other material.

Morehead, Joe. 1999. *Introduction to United States Government
Information*, 6th ed. Englewood, CO: Libraries Unlimited, Inc.

Last published in 1999, it remains one of the classic reference guides to
the basics of government documents and related information. Morehead
covers cataloging, periodical indexes, the legislative process, legal publishing, copyrights, patents, maps, and more.

Morrison, Andrea M., ed. 2008. *Managing Electronic Government
Information in Libraries: Issues and Practices.* Chicago, IL: American
Library Association.

Chapters are written by government information professionals, addressing issues related to understanding and managing government and
government-related electronic resources and topics: technology, collection management, diverse populations and access to information (the
digital divide), information literacy and instruction, and preservation. It
also includes advice and best practices for managing collections in the
digital age.

Morrison, Andrea M., and Barbara J. Mann. 2004. *International
Government Information and Country Information: A Subject Guide.*
Westport, CT: Greenwood Press.

This is an essential guide to international agencies, including the European Union and the United Nations. Non-governmental organizations
(NGOs), such as Doctors Without Borders and the Gates Foundation,
and intergovernmental organizations (IGOs), such as development
banks and trade organizations, are also covered extensively.

## ELECTRONIC DISCUSSION LISTS, BLOGS, AND PROFESSIONAL ORGANIZATIONS

Here is an overview of resources most used by government information librarians. (See Chapter 3 for more links and descriptions.)

FDLP Desktop, www.fdlp.gov. For librarians working in FDLP libraries
this is the principal resource, beginning with the GovDocs Quick-

start Guide. It describes the basics of being a depository library and spells out the legal and other requirements of the program. The site also includes in-depth information and links to collection tools, cataloging, and Superintendent of Documents (SuDocs) Classification. Users can also easily connect to the FDLP for guidance and answers to questions. The GPO staff is very responsive to questions from the FDLP community.

GOVDOC-L is the discussion list used by librarians and personnel who are part of the FDLP. I have found this to be one of the best online groups in which to participate. It is a very active group of generous and tenacious librarians who never give up trying to find elusive documents and related information and gladly direct you to resources you did not know about. You can sign up as soon as you notify the FDLP that you are the new librarian in charge of your library's government information depository. I have posted queries here many times and have always received very detailed and helpful responses. It is a great feeling when you know enough to answer questions, too.

GODORT, www.wikis.ala.org/godort. ALA's Government Documents Round Table is another essential resource for new and established government information librarians. Especially helpful are the "toolboxes" for processing and cataloging state, local, federal, and international government documents. The GODORT Education Committee is also active in helping with training and marketing government information resources. A variety of helpful information is available at http://wikis.ala.org/godort/index.php/Exchange.

MAGIRT, www.ala.org/magirt, is ALA's Map and Geospatial Information Round Table. MAGIRT will help you with issues related to print and electronic maps, including GIS training and resources. They also have guidelines about weeding and organizing map collections. GODORT and MAGIRT members are very knowledgeable about general federal government resources, and these two groups often get together. You do not need to join ALA to access their resources, but if you are part of the FDLP and an ALA member these are two key user groups.

"Help! I'm an Accidental Government Information Librarian" webinars are free and easy to access from the North Carolina Library Association website, www.nclaonline.org/government-resources. They cover a wide variety of topics, and the webinars are usually a half hour in length, with additional time for Q&A with the presenters. Recorded sessions are available after the webinars are presented, and all are currently available on YouTube by searching "Help! I'm an Accidental Government Information Librarian Webinars." Begun in 2011, this series presents webinars featuring many kinds of resources and information and are a wonderful resource for new and established government information librarians. If you have a special area of expertise, you can conduct a webinar too. I have done one myself and really enjoyed the experience and the feedback.

*Government Info Pro,* www.governmentinfopro.com, is a blog from LexisNexis and a free online resource posting articles, commentary, and advice for everyone in the government information community. A key feature is the series Best Practices for Government Libraries that includes articles and advice from library and legal sources. The entire annual Best Practices series can be downloaded in PDF format.

*Free Government Information,* http://freegovinfo.info, is a blog for librarians, journalists, researchers, and others to post and discuss government-related topics. Its mission is to make sure that all citizens have free access to information and resources and that these resources are preserved and easily accessible.

## Journals

*DttP: Documents to the People* is the official publication of GODORT and is published quarterly by the American Library Association. This journal covers issues related to technical and public services topics. Content is also available online for GODORT members through the GODORT wiki link, http://wikis.ala.org/godort/index.php/DttP _Full_Text.

*Government Information Quarterly* is a peer-reviewed journal covering policies, practices, resources, and services of the document community. It contains many useful articles on best practices and scholarship on historic and current documents-related issues. It is available online from Elsevier through EBSCO and Science Direct Journals.

*State and Local Government Review* is an e-journal published three times a year and is available through SAGE Publications. The official journal of the Section on Intergovernmental Administration &

Management (SIAM) of the American Society for Public Administration (ASPA), it brings public administrators and academics together to identify and focus on state and local government policies and issues.

## Websites

**LibGuides Community,** http://libguides.com/community. You do not have to be a subscriber to LibGuides to access these guides, and it is a great place to find out what other government information librarians are highlighting as resources for their users. There are many course-specific guides included, so if you are teaching a similar instruction session you have many good resources to check out. Here are some LibGuides I find to be particularly helpful:

- Government Information on the Web Subject Index, http://lib.stmarytx.edu/govsub, is a very comprehensive A-Z list of government information resources available from the US government and other institutions.
- GovSpeak, http://libguides.ucsd.edu/govspeak, lists what all those hundreds of government acronyms mean.
- List of Foreign Governments, http://libguides.northwestern.edu/ForeignGovernmentList, is an alphabetical listing by country of government departments and related sites (e.g., banks, trade missions, etc.).

**WorldCat.org,** www.worldcat.org, is a great place to find materials held at libraries around the world. I often recommend this for scholarly and legal research if my library's collection does not contain what users are seeking. WorldCat also has digitized resources that can be downloaded.

**Useful Websites for Documents Librarians,** http://lib.law.washington.edu/ref/docsweb.html, is compiled by Peggy Jarrett at the University of Washington's Gallagher Law Library. Many of these links are covered in greater depth in Chapters 3 and 4.

**two**

# The Federal Depository
# Library Program (FDLP)

This chapter covers the FDLP and your library's role in it. The history, basics, and future directions of the program are also covered here. Chapter 5 contains more detailed information about the issues, challenges, and opportunities currently facing the FDLP and the GPO.

## A BRIEF HISTORY OF THE FDLP AND THE GPO

The FDLP was established by Congressional resolution in 1813 to ensure the American public free and open access to US government information. The resolution designated that a single copy of all Senate and House documents be sent to each college, university, or historical society of each state and territory in the United States. Though the program has changed and evolved, the primary mission remains the same: that documents distributed by the US government in print and electronic formats are free of charge to the public and are easily accessible in regional and selective repository libraries. Ideally, these libraries are staffed by personnel who are well-versed in government documents and are readily available to help citizens get the information they need.

The Printing Act of 1852 established the position of Superintendent of Public Printing, later to become the Public Printer. It also established elections of public printers for the House and Senate and created the Joint Committee on Printing (JCP) to ensure that printing was seamless and consistent between both chambers. In 1857, depository designation and distribution guidelines were placed under the Secretary of the Interior, and depository library designation expanded to include different types of libraries, such as law and tribal libraries. In 1858, Congress passed legislation allowing each state representative and territorial delegate to designate depository libraries in the areas they represented, and in 1859 the Senate gained the authority to designate one depository library in their states. The most current regulations and legal obligations of the FDLP can be found in the United States Code, chapters 1901–1916 (44 USC §§1901–1916).

In 1861, Congress officially established the Government Printing Office (GPO). Prior to that time most government documents were printed by private companies, the contracts of which were often influenced by political concerns and were plagued by cronyism, inconsistencies, and inefficiencies. The official history of the GPO states:

> By the mid-19th century...the high costs, ineffective service, and repeated scandals of contract printing made it clear that the needs of the growing Nation could no longer be satisfied by that system. In its place Congress established the Government Printing Office, and this effort was rewarded almost immediately with a reduction in costs, vastly improved service, and the elimination of scandal. (US Government Printing Office, 2011b)

Major improvements in service, quality, and timeliness of printing were quickly apparent. In 1869, the GPO created the position of Superintendent of Documents who was responsible for distributing documents to federal depository libraries.

By 1873, the GPO handled the printing for all three branches of the federal government and established the printing of the *Congressional Record*, the daily accounting of Congressional proceedings and debates. The GPO also established a unit at the Library of Congress to help library personnel handle government documents. In 1895, the Superintendent of Documents was relocated from the Department of the Interior to the GPO, with additional duties that included the sale of documents. Librarian Adelaide Rosalie Hasse was recruited from the Los Angeles Public Library to tackle the problem of bibliographic control, and she laid the foundation of SuDoc classification for government documents that continues to this day (Ennis, 2007).

## GPO'S "BORN DIGITAL" DOCUMENTS AND AUTHENTICATION

Ushering in the digital age, 1993's Government Printing Office Electronic Information Act (P.L. 103-40) was the basis for GPO Access, the first easily accessible and searchable online portal to government documents. Established in 1994, this site provided permanent access to electronic documents issued by the three branches of the federal government. It is estimated that users have downloaded more than a billion documents from this site (US Government Printing Office, 2011b). GPO Access was phased out in 2011, and all the documents were transitioned to FDsys.gov. The reason for this change was to incorporate enhancements allowing users easier access to all government publications. Users can also perform more complex searches with quicker results, use help tools and tutorials, download content more easily, and be assured that all the documents are authenticated. Note that while GPO Access is no longer available, some content is archived and available through the Internet Archive's Wayback Machine.

GPO has worked hard to incorporate new technologies to make much of its content electronic, or "born digital." Paradoxically, while making it more convenient for users to access government information, it has also created an identity crisis for the GPO and the FDLP. To put it simply, what is the point of having a print distribution program if most of its content is freely available electronically, either through FDsys, individual government department and agency sites, or for-profit and free websites such as Google, HathiTrust, and the Internet Archive? In addition, to cut down on both the time and personnel needed to get documents cataloged and shelved, many selectives are currently dropping print resources from their FDLP item selection in favor of receiving and cataloging only electronic documents. (See Chapter 3 for more about managing digital resources and Chapter 5 for a broader look at this issue.)

Authentication is one of the key features of GPO's born-digital documents. In its 2011 whitepaper, *Authenticity of Electronic Federal Government Publications*, the GPO outlined the steps it has taken to ensure that content of each document is whole and has not been altered in any way. For those concerned that future file formats may cause current formats to become obsolete, the report states that the GPO will strive to move all content to the most current file formats (US Government Printing Office, 2011a). It is unclear at this time whether documents from agencies and departments outside the GPO will have similar file format upgrades or contain any kind of official authentication.

## THE DEPOSITORY LIBRARY COUNCIL AND FDLP ANNUAL MEETINGS

The Depository Library Council (DLC) to the Public Printer was established in 1972 to provide advice on policy matters related to the FDLP. The council currently consists of fifteen members who are either current or former depository librarians. The primary focus of the DLC's work is to advise the Public Printer, the Superintendent of Documents, and members of the GPO staff on how to maintain and modernize the efficient management of the FDLP.

The FDLP typically holds its meetings at the GPO headquarters in Washington, DC, or at a nearby location. The meetings are attended by government documents librarians, the DLC, representatives from the GPO, government information print and database vendors, and others involved in the government information community. At these meetings, workshops and training sessions focus on topics relevant to regionals and selectives; for example, managing collections in the digital age, weeding collections, and marketing government information. The DLC meets daily in an open forum to discuss issues affecting member libraries, such as funding, trends in government information, and the impact of Congressional and Executive action (or inaction), such as sequestration, upcoming legislation, and any other changes that could impact repositories and selectives on the state level. Until 2013 there were annual spring and fall meetings, but due to the government shutdown in fall 2013 the fall meeting was postponed until spring 2014. In 2015 the FDLP once again held its annual fall meeting and included a concurrent virtual meeting for those who couldn't attend in person.

Attending these meetings is a good way to touch base with and learn from your fellow librarians and other government information professionals. If you do attend, note that registration is free but transportation and hotel costs must be covered by you or your library. If you cannot attend in person you can register for virtual meeting sessions, and most of the poster sessions and presentations are posted to the FDLP Desktop site before and after the event.

## REGIONAL AND SELECTIVE FEDERAL DEPOSITORY LIBRARIES

There are currently 1,158 FDLs in the United States and US territories. Forty-seven of these are regionals, with the balance being selectives. Academic libraries make up more than half of all FDLs, with the rest divided among law, public, government, state, corporate, and tribal libraries. While most states have at least one regional library, there are now eight states that no longer do. Some are sharing with a regional located in another state in their geographic area, but others are still waiting to find out if they can become part of a multi-state consortium. (See Chapter 5 for a discussion about the issues facing states that no longer have regional libraries.)

Regional depository libraries, typically located in large state universities or state capitol libraries, receive one hundred percent of government documents distributed by the GPO in print, microform, CD-ROMs, DVDs, or online formats. Depositories are required by the FDLP to keep these resources in perpetuity, however there are some exceptions: superseded documents can be discarded and some may be removed through weeding. As of 2015 the GPO has issued a new Regional Depository Library Discard Policy, which outlines updated processes and best practices to streamline discards and make sure that there will be tangible copies available in case of disaster or other issues that impede access to documents (Baish and Etkin, 2015).

Selective depository libraries include academic, public, law, government, and special libraries. If your library is a selective the collection most likely reflects the particular areas of interest to your state, local area, or research priorities. For example, if your library is located in a state with agricultural and mining interests, the majority of your documents probably originate from the Departments of Agriculture and the Interior. Having a good understanding of the range of your collection helps you to better serve the needs of your users, and if these needs change, you can easily update your collection profile. Regional depositories offer support to selectives through consultation and help with collection and weeding issues. Many state repositories and selectives are also putting together state plans to facilitate more collaborative efforts at both the state and national level. Get to know the personnel at the regional depository library serving your area, and keep their contact information handy when you need guidance. Regionals and selectives must comply with the legal requirements found in 44 USC §§1901 1916 to remain members in good standing with the program and can be put on probationary status if they are found to be non-compliant.

## THE FDLP AND YOU

Ideally, you were able to meet with your predecessor to go over the essentials of managing the collection or there was a good paper trail for you to follow if that person had left.

At the most basic level, you should know:

* Your institution's depository number
* How to update your institution's contact information
* Whom to contact at your regional depository (if you are a selective)
* Where to find copies of previous Biennial Surveys
* If and when your library last had an official FDLP site inspection

This information should also be on file with your library administration. Make sure you notify your library administration when you make changes to your basic information or collection profile.

The FDLP Desktop site, www.fdlp.gov, is your source for the latest updates on collection management, basic and essential titles, preservation, and special events such as national and regional meetings. You can easily link to the *FDLP Handbook, Selection Profile*, the *Catalog of U.S. Publications*, and other resources from this site. Libraries that have some government documents but are not part of the FDLP can still access FDLP Desktop as there is no password needed. They can also order materials from the GPO to add to or update their collections, but as non-members they must pay for them.

Starting in 2016, a Coordinator Certificate Program consisting of eight online courses led by GPO personnel and conducted through the FDLP Academy Training Assistance Center will be available for new documents librarians. The program covers the basics of managing a federal depository collection, and participants will participate in weekly readings, discussions, webinars, and quizzes. More information about this program can be found on the FDLP.gov site.

## GOVERNMENT INFORMATION COLLECTION MUST HAVES: "BASIC COLLECTION" AND "ESSENTIAL TITLES"

The "Basic Collection" includes those titles that every FDL is required by the GPO to have in its collection and be available for immediate use. Since many of these titles are available in electronic format it usually is not necessary to have the most current versions of them in print as well. While the list is subject to change, as of 2015 it contains twenty titles and includes publications of all three branches of government: Legislative, Executive, and Judicial. Titles include the *Code of Federal Regulations, Daily Compilation of Presidential Documents, American FactFinder, Ben's Guide to the U.S. Government*, the *Congressional Record, Economic Indicators*, and more. The entire list, with links to full-text, can be accessed from the FDLP.gov site by searching "FDLP Basic Collection."

"Essential Titles" are items chosen by the depository community as those that every FDL should, but are not officially required, to have. Some of these titles overlap with the basic list, but additional titles have been included. One of the main purposes of this list is to make sure that each library has the same reference works that have been identified as key resources for reference and research. The Essential Titles collection, developed in 1977 by the DLC, initially consisted of twenty-three reference titles and was included in the council's 1977 publication *Guidelines for the Depository Library System*. As of 2015, this collection contains thirty-nine titles and is subject to change depending on the acquisition or loss of publications from the issuing agencies. The complete Essential Titles list is accessible from the FDLP.gov site. As with the basic list, titles come from all three branches of government and include the *Budget of the United States, House and Senate Journals, The Code of Federal Regulations, The Federal Register, United States Code, Statutes at Large, Agricultural Statistics*, various Census reports, Supreme Court decisions, presidential papers, various congressional publications (reports, hearings, etc.), *The World Factbook*, and more.

The contents of most of these titles are available online in digitized and searchable full-text formats through the government websites FDsys and Congress.gov. FDsys will be replaced by govinfo.gov, which is currently in beta. Search engines such as Google and Google Scholar and databases such as ProQuest's *Congressional* and *Statistical Insight, Hein Online*, the HathiTrust, and Internet Archive are also good places to find abstracts and full-text government information. Not all content has been digitized, however, so be sure to look at the dates of coverage for specific resources. For example, the digitized *Statutes at Large*, accessible from FDsys, only goes back to 1951; print resources from your collection or from another FDL would be needed to cover prior statutes. Digitization of government documents is ongoing at many research libraries, so use Google or the LibGuides Community site to see who might have more historic content available. The GPO is also partnering with a number of depository libraries on digitization projects.

## BIENNIAL SURVEY AND LIBRARY NEEDS ASSESSMENT

Every two years the FDLP issues an online survey that must be filled out completely and returned to the FDLP by every repository and selective. It covers all aspects of your government information collection: the overall count of print and online items; piece-level cataloging procedures; the condition and preservation of the print collection; emergency and disaster planning; and weeding efforts. The survey also asks if your library plans to stay in the program. In 2015, the Library Needs Assessment section was added to the Biennial Survey so that the GPO and Superintendent of Documents could get a clearer picture of current conditions and future needs of FDLs. A sample survey is available for you to download and fill out before you complete the actual survey, and I strongly recommend that you do this as it may take some time to find all the answers. It is also helpful to refer back to your library's previous surveys if they are available. Before the survey is submitted your library director or other approving officer in library administration must review and sign off on it, so make sure to build in time to do this. The survey must also be submitted to your state or regional repository librarian(s), and you can email it to both your regional and the FDLP at the same time. Download and save a copy of the completed survey to have it available for someone filling out the next Biennial Survey if you are no longer the coordinator.

If you have any questions about the survey, contact your state repository for guidance and check the FDLP.gov site for FAQs and ongoing discussions regarding the survey.

## ON-SITE INSPECTIONS

In the past, the GPO conducted periodic on-site inspections, but the Biennial Survey is currently the main instrument now used to gather information about individual FDLs. If your library previously had any on-site inspections, however, the resulting reports will indicate how the collection was evaluated and what recommendations were made. Check with your library administration to find out if these recommendations were carried out. I have converted my library's previous inspection reports to PDFs and placed them in the library's shared drive to make sure they are available for everyone to see. Even though official inspections are no longer conducted by the GPO, the collection still should be evaluated periodically by you and other library personnel. See suggestions for checking the collection in Chapter 3.

## LEAVING OR STAYING AS A MEMBER OF THE FDLP

While there is a more in-depth discussion about this issue in Chapter 5, I also want to touch on it here. Many libraries are weighing the benefits and drawbacks of staying in the FDLP, and your library administration may be taking a critical look at maintaining its role as a regional or selective FDL.

The following are some of the most common questions being asked by many library administrators:

- Why are we processing tangible documents when it takes up valuable time and personnel that could be better utilized elsewhere?
- Can the library stop downloading cataloging records to the local OPAC and just have them be available through a "discovery" platform?
- Isn't everything online now and therefore freely available?
- Can the library get all of its basic and essential government documents in electronic format only and still be part of the program?
- Can the library remain in the FDLP if it discontinues receiving any print and electronic documents?
- Is there an ongoing weeding program in place? If not, what is the process we need to follow?
- What does the library need to do to get out of the program altogether?

The last question is a major one faced by many FDLs. If a library does decide to leave the program it involves a lot of planning, time commitment, and personnel from all areas of the library. The accounts of those who have gone through this process are very helpful (Kownslar, 1999; McKenzie, Gemellaro, and Walters, 2000). Additionally, there is a lot of discussion in the government information community about Congressional initiatives regarding funding, or lack of it, for GPO, FDLP, and FDsys. The GPO and GODORT discussion lists have very active forums on these issues, so make it a priority to monitor or play an active part in these ongoing conversations. Do not be blindsided if you are asked to make changes to your own program, or if you find that access to certain resources is no longer freely available.

## THE FDLP COMMUNITY

As mentioned in previous chapters, I strongly recommend getting to know other documents librarians at the local, state, and national level. They can work with you on issues you may encounter in your new role and advise you on collection management. They can also help you become familiar with regional and national issues affecting government information librarians and generally offer support and guidance. Going to the national FDLP meetings is a good way to meet people with similar interests and put faces to names that often come up in articles and websites. Documents librarians actively participate in discussion lists, training, and outreach and keep current on new government and related resources. If you are working in a small library or in an area with few or no other FDLs it is especially important to network through the FDLP community. If you are in a large metropolitan area with different kinds of selective libraries you may want to meet face-to-face periodically with your fellow librarians to discuss issues, training opportunities, and other things you have in common.

## FUTURE DIRECTIONS FOR THE FDLP AND GPO

GPO's Superintendent of Documents unveiled the *National Plan for the Future of the FDLP* at the spring 2014 FDLP meeting, and implementation of the plan was a major topic at the 2015 meeting. The vision is "to provide Government information when and where it is needed" (Baish and Etkin, 2014). To achieve this goal, the major priorities are to: implement the regional depository discard policy; continue to add pre-1976 cataloging records; work with regionals on cataloging and metadata partnerships; move from a print-centric operation to one that is content-centric; design, or redesign, user interfaces for user-centric access; expand web harvesting; digitize the historical collections of Government publications; and seek to expand access to attract more users. The GPO is also working to revise the *Legal Requirements and Program Regulations of the Federal Depository Library Program*. However, the national plan does not really address the fundamental issue of whether the FDLP is still viable overall when access to digital government resources is easily available through FDsys, government agencies, Google, and other search engines.

In 2014, Congress approved legislation to allow the GPO to change its name from the Government Printing Office to the Government *Publishing* Office, reflecting the larger scope of what the GPO does beyond print production, and, in particular, providing access to digital content through FDsys, e-books, and apps.

In 2012, the FDLP sent a questionnaire to the FDLP community regarding state focused action plans (SFAPs). Respondents were asked to provide up to five initiatives and activities they planned to take in the next five years. Forty states and territories submitted thirty-four SFAPs, and the final report, *State Focused Action Plans: FDLP Forecast Study*, was released in 2013 listing the highlights of each state's plan. Three areas in particular—promoting awareness of collections, increasing interlibrary loans, and identifying publications for digitization—were named as important areas that states and regional FDLs wanted to work on. Simplified weeding procedures was also listed as a major interest of respondents. While these plans have been discussed within the FDLP community and at state, regional, and annual meetings, there has not been a unified effort to act on them, but some states and regionals are proceeding with their own projects.

## References

Baish, Mary Alice, and Cindy Etkin. 2014. National Plan for the Future of the FDLP. www.fdlp.gov/file-repository/outreach/events/depository-library-council -dlc-meetings/2014-meeting-proceedings/2462-national-plan-for-the-future -of-the-fdlp/file.

Baish, Mary Alice, and Cindy Etkin. 2015. New Regional Depository Library Discard Policy. www.fdlp.gov/file-repository/outreach/events/depository-library-council-dlc -meetings/2015-meeting-proceedings-1/2015-dlc-meeting-and-fdl-conference/2661 -new-regional-depository-library-discard-policy/file.

Ennis, Lisa A. 2007. *Government Documents Librarianship: A Guide to the Neo-depository Era.* Medford, NJ: Information Today, Inc., 9-13.

Kownslar, Edward. 1999. "Closing Down a Government Documents Collection: The Experiences of Millsaps College." *DttP: Documents to the People* 27, no. 4: 11–12.

McKenzie, Elizabeth M., Elizabeth Gemellaro, and Carolyn Walters. 2000. "Leaving Paradise: Dropping Out of the Federal Depository Library Program." *Law Library Journal* 92, no. 3: 305–319. www.aallnet.org/main-menu/Publications/llj/LLJ -Archives/Vol-92/pub_llj_v92n03/2000-27.pdf.

US Government Printing Office. 2011a. *Authenticity of Electronic Federal Government Publications.* Washington, DC: GPO. www.gpo.gov/pdfs/authentication/authenti cationwhitepaper2011.pdf.

US Government Printing Office. 2011b. *Keeping America Informed. The U.S. Government Printing Office: 150 Years of Service to the Nation.* Washington, DC: US Government Printing Office: 133. www.gpo.gov/fdsys/pkg/GPO -KEEPINGAMERICAINFORMED/pdf.

## Recommended Reading

American Association of Law Libraries. 2011. *AALL Federal Legislative Advocacy Update: GPO Funding.* http://aallwash.wordpress.com/2011/09/17/aall-federal -legislative-advocacy-update-gpo-funding.

Association of Research Libraries. 2011. *ARL Statement on Recent USGPO Decisions Concerning the FDLP.* www.arl.org/bm~doc/fdlp_arlstatement_12oct11.pdf.

Baish, Mary Alice, Laurie Hall, and Cindy Etkin. 2015. *Implementing the National Plan: Focusing on Users and Services.* www.fdlp.gov/file-repository/outreach/events/ depository-library-council-dlc-meetings/2015-meeting-proceedings-1/2015-dlc -meeting-and-fdl-conference/2658-implementing-the-national-plan-focusing-on -users-and-services/file.

Braunstein, Stephanie A., Fang H. Gao, and Joseph R. Nicholson. 2013. "What's Up with Docs?!? The Peculiarities of Cataloging Federal Government Serial Publications." *The Serials Librarian: From the Printed Page to the Digital Age* 64, no. 1–4: 235–244. http://dx.doi.org/10.1080/0361526X.2013.760416.

Federal Depository Library Program. 2011. *About the FDLP.* www.fdlp.gov/home/about.

Federal Depository Library Program. 2013. *State Focused Action Plans.* http://tinyurl.com/stateactionplan.

Jacobs, Jim, and Melody Kelly. "The Future of the FDLP: From Conversation to Confrontation." *Library Journal,* December 13, 2011. http://lj.libraryjournal.com/2011/12/opinion/backtalk/the-future-of-the-fdlp-from-conversation-to-confrontation.

Jacobs, James A. "Privatization of GPO, Defunding of FDsys, and the Future of the FDLP." *Free Government Information (FGI),* August 11, 2011. http://freegovinfo.info/node/3416.

Jacobs, James A., James R. Jacobs, and Shinjoung Yeo. 2005. "Government Information in the Digital Age: The Once and Future Federal Depository Library Program." *The Journal of Academic Librarianship* 31, no. 3: 198–208.

Jaeger, Paul T., John C. Bertot, and John A. Shuler. 2010. "The Federal Depository Library Program (FDLP), Academic Libraries, and Access to Government Information." *The Journal of Academic Librarianship* 36, no. 6: 469–478. doi:10.1016/j.acalib.2010.08.002.

Keiser, Barbie E. "GPO Disapproves of Report on the Future of Federal Depository Libraries." *Information Today,* August 25, 2011. http://newsbreaks.infotoday.com/NewsBreaks/GPO-Disapproves-of-Report-on-the-Future-of-Federal-Depository-Libraries-77289.asp.

Seavey, Charles A. 2005. "Documents to the People." *American Libraries* 36, no 7: 42–44.

Seavey, Charles A. 2010. "GPO Must Go: The Government Printing Office is an Obsolete Relic." *American Libraries* 41, no. 10: 33. http://freegovinfo.info/files/Seavey-gpo-must-go.pdf.

Selby, Barbie. 2008. "Age of Aquarius—The FDLP in the 21st century." *Government Information Quarterly* 25, no. 1: 38–47. www.sciencedirect.com/science/article/pii/S0740624X07000810.

Sowell, Steven L., Michael H. Boock, Lawrence A. Landis, and Jennifer E. Nutefall. 2012. "Between a Rock and a Hard Place: Managing Government Document Collections in a Digital World." *Collection Management* 37, no. 2: 98–109. http://ir.library.oregonstate.edu/xmlui/bitstream/handle/1957/28809/Between_a_rock_and_a_hard_place.pdf?sequence=1.

Walsh, John. 2008. "Who Will Be Responsible? The Authentication and Preservation of Government Digital Information." *Library Hi Tech News* 25, no. 9: 22–25. http://dx.doi.org/10.1108/07419050810946222.

**three**

# Managing the Collection

This chapter covers the management of the print and electronic resources in your collection. Whether you do all the processing, cataloging, and shelving of items in the collection or if these functions are currently being handled by other departments in the library, the following resources will give you a clearer understanding of the terminology and procedures unique to maintaining government information collections. If staff in other departments are handling the processing of government resources, set up appointments to speak with them about the workflow involved with getting items added to or removed from the collection. It also will help you get to know staff you will need to work with if any problems should arise.

## SuDoc CLASSIFICATION

US government documents have their own classification system, SuDoc (Superintendent of Documents). Here are some resources to help you understand how it works.

**Learning SuDoc Call Numbers,** www.lib.msu.edu/branches/gov/for-libns.

> Includes a call number quiz and shelving exercises that are very helpful for personnel and students who work with government documents.

Superintendent of Documents (SuDoc) Classification Scheme, www.fdlp .gov/22-about/services/929-sudoc-classification-scheme.

Contains current lettering for SuDoc class stems and guidance from the FDLP. An earlier version, from the GODORT toolbox wiki, is also helpful: http://tinyurl.com/lppjfzf.

## RESOURCES AVAILABLE THROUGH FDLP DESKTOP

GovDocs Quickstart Guide, www.fdlp.gov/govdocs-quickstart-guide.

The information here will help you understand the fundamentals of managing the collection. It is especially important to let the GPO know right away that you are now the contact so that you can receive updates, discussion list messages, and other vital information as soon as possible.

Requirements and Guidance, www.fdlp.gov/requirements-guidance/ guidance.

The Guidance tab contains a comprehensive index of links to help you understand the FDLP's regulations and legal requirements. It is very important to familiarize yourself with these obligations and discuss them with library administration if any questions arise about the status and condition of the collection.

Federal Depository Library Program Tools, www.fdlp.gov/about-the-fdlp/ federal-depositorylibraries.

The general URL provides information on FDLP repositories and selectives. Managers of selectives can learn what items are currently being selected for their collection, and review collection and item selection profiles, by going to the FDLP Desktop, and selecting Item Lister under Collection Tools, https://selections.fdlp.gov/OA_HTML/gpolibItemLis ter.jsp. This shows not only the items in the library's collection, but also provides comparison information on other repositories and selectives similar in size and focus.

GOVDOC-L, http://govdoc-l.org.

For new documents librarians this is the essential users group. You should also sign up for your state and local government information discussion lists if they are available.

## RESOURCES AVAILABLE THROUGH GPO.GOV

**FDsys,** www.gpo.gov/fdsys.

Online tutorials and webinars are available on how best to use and search these resources.

*Catalog of U.S. Government Publications,* http://catalog.gpo.gov/ F?RN=514442325.

This is the GPO's finding tool for locating federal publications from 1976 to the present. To search for items published prior to 1976, you will need to go to the print copies of the *Monthly Catalog of U.S. Government Publications,* SuDoc GP 3.8/7 or, if you have access, use ProQuest's *Monthly Catalog of U.S. Government Publications, 1895-1976.* This is the best place to look if patrons know the title or year of publication of the documents they need. The Internet Archive also has some digitized volumes of the monthly catalog available.

## RESOURCES AVAILABLE THROUGH THE GODORT WIKI

**Toolbox for Processing and Cataloging Federal Government Documents,** http://wikis.ala.org/godort/index.php/Toolbox_for_Processing_and _Cataloging_Federal_Government_Documents.

This is an invaluable resource with links to all the essential tools you will need, many connecting to the FDLP Desktop and the Documents Data Miner 2 (DDM2) sites. Make sure to look at:

* The List of Classes, containing the official listing of publications available for selection by participating FDLPs from each government agency. The list includes the item numbers and all the formats available for each item.
* WEBTech Notes highlighting updates to the List of Classes and class changes
* Shipping List information
* Toolboxes for International and State and Local documents processing and cataloging

## DOCUMENTS DATA MINER 2

Hosted by the University of Wichita, the Documents Data Miner 2 (DDM2), http://govdoc.wichita.edu/ddm2/gdocframes.asp.

Works in conjunction with the GPO and FDLP to identify the item numbers that each depository selects. All you need to know is your depository number to get started. The DDM database can be searched by title, SuDoc or item number, agency, and more (Ennis, 2007).

In DDM2, you and your cataloging staff can also:

- Find out the percentage of documents your library receives from specific agencies
- Find out the SuDoc stem assigned to each item number and the exact publication title
- Locate "Inactive and Discontinued Items"
- Download MARC records
- Download reports from DDM2 to Excel spreadsheets

## GUIDES FOR MANAGING ELECTRONIC COLLECTIONS

As mentioned in Chapter 2, these are two very good guides to help you understand the essentials of collection management in the digital age:

Ennis, Lisa A. 2007. *Government Documents Librarianship: A Guide to the Neo-depositing Era*. Medford, NJ: Information Today, Inc.

This guide is especially useful for new depository librarians learning how to manage tangible and digital resources. Ennis covers all the nuts and bolts of collection management, with the focus on electronic resources, and also suggests ways to market government information collections. Chapter 8, dealing with technical services issues, such as cataloging and bibliographic control, processing, and preservation of tangible items, is particularly helpful for librarians who do not normally do cataloging or processing. The book also includes several very helpful appendices that include additional resources, a Self-Study template, and a sample of a Biennial Survey.

Morrison, Andrea M., ed. 2008. *Managing Electronic Government Information in Libraries: Issues and Practices*. Chicago, IL: American Library Association.

The chapters are written by government information professionals, addressing issues related to understanding and managing government and government-related electronic resources and topics: technology, collection management, diverse populations and access to information, information literacy and instruction, digital preservation, and more. It also includes a lot of advice and resources for best practices on managing collections in the digital age.

These guides are full of practical information and will really help you become more comfortable with collection management in general. There are also timely articles and reports available in *Government Information Quarterly* and other journals and blogs that deal with management and coordination issues.

## COLLECTION DEVELOPMENT POLICY

The FDLP strongly suggests that libraries develop and follow a collection development policy. If your library already has a written policy for the government information collection, check to see that it is up to date. If not, make changes that cover your current situation. If there has never been an established policy, check with library administration and the departments in the library to see if they have suggestions or can direct you to policies set up for other collections. The policy should cover:

* The collection of Basic and Essential titles (see Chapter 2)
* Items most needed by your user population (census data, tax forms, etc.)
* What kinds of selection tools to use (*Catalog of U.S. Government Publications*, websites, other sources)
* Setting up a periodic review of the tangible collection (superseded items, shelf reading, weeding, etc.)
* Conducting periodic reviews of persistent uniform resource locator (PURLs), i.e., check for any broken links or other issues that limit access
* Gathering and posting usage statistics from electronic resources (specify the process by which it is done and who is responsible for it, if not you)
* Spelling out the details of any consortium arrangements with other regionals and selectives in the same state or geographic location
* Updating contact information for key personnel at regional libraries, the GPO, and FDLP
* Scheduling and preparing the Biennial Survey
* Setting policies for access issues—ADA-compliance, hours of operation, etc.
* Guidelines for weeding and handling superseded items

There may be other policy issues specific to your particular library that you want to include, too. As an example, the University of Chicago collection development policy is very comprehensive: http://guides.lib.uchicago.edu/content.php?pid=273342&sid=3793074.

## PROCESSING INCOMING ITEMS

Each month, the GPO ships tangible items and provides links to electronic resources to all of its repositories and selectives. You and any library personnel working with these documents should consult the shipping lists that come with each delivery to make sure everything was received correctly. If there are any discrepancies with receiving or not receiving the materials you regularly order, you should contact the GPO as soon as possible and arrange to have the incorrect items shipped back or have them ship any missing items to you. The FDLP suggests keeping shipping lists for at least three years because it is a good way to monitor what you receive and to keep a paper trail for others to check if you are not available. After the items are unpacked, you or your cataloging department must handle processing items at the piece-level (individual item), according to FDLP guidelines. Tangible items, including kits, must be labeled by SuDoc number (or other classification if the items are being placed in the general collection), and barcoded before being shelved.

Repositories and selectives can download cataloging records via the monthly catalog of documents and by creating their own labels and barcodes, but many choose to do it through MARCIVE, Inc. (http://home.marcive.com). In partnership with the GPO, MARCIVE has a program in place to handle monthly processing of government information in tangible and electronic formats. Through MARCIVE, your library receives shipping lists, cataloging records, and labels and barcodes for tangible items. If your library already uses MARCIVE for processing the general collection's cataloging records and related services, processing of government documents is an additional service.

## SHELVING AND STORING TANGIBLE ITEMS

Many, but not all, libraries keep government documents in an area separate from the general collection, shelved in SuDoc order. All tangible items, including bound volumes, periodicals, brochures, maps, microfiche, kits, and CD-ROMs are usually placed in appropriate shelving, drawers, paper or plastic files (e.g., Princeton files), and cabinets specifically used to house these collections.

However, there are FDLs that shelve their tangible government documents with the general library collection, either under Library of Congress Classification (LCC) for academic and law libraries or Dewey Decimal Classification (DDC) for public libraries. This arrangement allows patrons to more conveniently search for and discover government information. However, it is important that the MARC record contain both the SuDoc and LCC or DDC classification because if and when your library needs to pull superseded items, move the collection to off-site storage, or no longer participate in the FDLP, these items can quickly be moved off the shelves and deleted from the catalog easily as the cataloger can search using more than one classification system.

## MAP COLLECTIONS

Most printed topographical maps come directly from the United States Geological Survey (USGS), not through the GPO, and come with their own shipping lists. These shipments are intermittent, with no particular delivery schedule. USGS has made most of their maps available online in digitized and fully searchable formats at www.usgs.gov. If you are weeding this collection, it is prudent to keep the tangible maps of your local, state, or regional areas so that researchers can find them quickly. You can also contact ALA's Map and Geospatial Round Table (MAGIRT), www.ala.org/magirt/front, for guidance on how to handle maps. Some libraries also get maps from the Central Intelligence Agency (CIA), local and state agencies, and, in the case of academic libraries, from earth sciences and geology department collections. Check with your acquisitions and cataloging departments to find out how to process these items.

## A CHECKLIST FOR EXAMINING YOUR TANGIBLE COLLECTION

As part of your collection policy you should set up a schedule to take a thorough look at the condition of your collection, whether it is in your library or in off-site storage. Also include others who are familiar with the collection, such as the shelving manager, so you can all keep notes.

Here are some questions to consider and act on as you walk around the stacks:

- Are the shelves neat and free of dust?
- Are the smaller pieces, such as brochures and unbound reports, located in paper or plastic files (Princeton files) or just placed haphazardly on the shelves?

- Are older books and printed pieces deteriorating, with loose or unglued bindings, yellowing or torn pages, etc.?
- Are there a series of unbound reports on the shelves that should go to the bindery?
- Does each item have the SuDoc number (or other classification) clearly marked?
- Does each item contain a bar code?
- Are items easy for all patrons to access or are they too high or low on the shelves?
- Is the collection ADA-compliant, and can patrons with disabilities move easily through the shelves, read the call numbers, and reach the materials they need?
- Are microfiche stored correctly in cabinets and in the proper SuDoc order?
- Are up-to-date microfiche readers readily available and close to the microfiche cabinets, preferably with printers attached?
- Are older CD-ROMs readable on your library's computer equipment?
- Are maps and larger items stored in horizontal map drawers? Are they easily accessible to patrons?
- Is there an FDLP sticker on the library's main entrance door and at the location of the collection? Is the FDLP logo displayed on your library's web page or Government Information online guide?
- Are there guides placed near the collection listing the SuDoc classification with signage indicating the SuDoc ranges of the items in each aisle?
- Is the shelving staff conducting periodical shelf reading and maintaining order? Are you coordinating this with the shelving manager?

If any of these areas need attention, speak with staff who can help you get these problems fixed in a timely manner. Keeping items in order and easily accessible makes the collection more inviting and useful to patrons. Having a clearer picture of the state of the collection will also help you fill out the Biennial Survey accurately.

## TAKING CARE OF OLDER ITEMS

If your library has been part of the FDLP for a long time, there may be items in the collection that are in fragile or deteriorating condition. Most common problems include: bindings coming unglued; mold; paper that is yellowing, tearing, or disintegrating; leather-bound books cracking; oversized items getting torn and bent; maps with rips and tears; yellowing or cracking tape on repaired items; and any other problems you might find. Check FDLP Physical Facilities, www.fdlp.gov/requirements-guidance-2/guidance/22-physical-facilities, for guidelines about preservation. If there is a special collections department in your library, ask the staff if they can help you assess the problems and find out if the most fragile items can be put in archival boxes and placed in a temperature- and humidity-controlled environment. If your library does not have anyone on the premises qualified to work with these items, check with your library administration to find out if you can get someone on an as-needed basis. You can also contact GPO and the FDLP for guidance.

## OFF-SITE STORAGE AND GOVERNMENT DOCUMENTS COLLECTIONS

Many libraries are moving some of their collections away from the main library to off-site storage. If your library is contemplating moving its government documents, it must work with the GPO to create a Selective Housing Agreement (SHA). This document:

> . . . outlines the partner's responsibilities to provide for free public access and also to maintain the records for and materials in the depository collection. The selective housing site . . . must display the FDLP eagle emblem on or near their entrance to demonstrate that the general public may access the FDLP collection housed at that site. (Federal Depository Library Program, 2014)

For more information on how to create and file an SHA, go to the FDLP Desktop site.

Documents that are placed in off-site storage may be vulnerable to water damage and mold. Prior to placing items in off-site storage, talk to the facilities manager about environmental issues and make sure that the facility has written contingency plans available in case mold or other damage occurs. Your state repository can also help with these issues and will let you dispose of damaged materials in accordance with your state and FDLP guidelines. You should also schedule a yearly visit to the off-site storage facility. It is important to remember that out of sight should not equal out of mind.

## WEEDING THE COLLECTION

It is important to remember that depository libraries do not own the federal documents in their collections—they remain the property of the federal government. Weeding any part of the collection can be a long and tedious project, especially if there are not enough people available to devote the time needed to pull items, prepare spreadsheets, arrange for shipping, remove records from the catalog, and take care of other details. To find out what to do, check Weeding a Depository Collection, www.fdlp.gov/requirements -guidance-2/guidance/30-weeding-a-depository-collection. Also contact your state or regional repository and ask for guidance on how best to proceed. The head of the repository will work with you to identify items for discard, how to set up lists, and how to safely discard the weeded items. If you are asked to weed large portions of your collection, identify the materials most requested in print by users. If these are unique to your collection or region, let library administration know why you are keeping them. Some of these materials are very difficult to replace.

### References

Ennis, Lisa A. 2007. *Government Documents Librarianship: A Guide to the Neo-depository Era.* Medford, NJ: Information Today, Inc., 76.

Federal Depository Library Program. 2014. Selective Housing Agreements (SHA). www.fdlp.gov/requirements-guidance-2/guidance/2007-selective-housing -agreements-sha.

**four**

# US Government
# and Related Sources

I have often heard the question, "Why should I go to government websites when all I need to do is Google my question?" Official US government and government-related sites (.gov, .org, .us, .edu) contain very useful information often beyond what the user was originally seeking, and they lead the user to verifiable and specific resources. Listed below are websites and databases that complement the government information you receive through the GPO.

## CITY, COUNTY, AND STATE SITES

Many citizens now access local and state government resources online. Typical searches include where and how to get different kinds of licenses, the location and hours of government offices, garbage and recycling pickup, zoning and property issues, emergency weather alerts, local demographic information, and more. GODORT's *Toolbox for Processing and Cataloging State and Local Government Documents* is a great resource to help manage and build your state and local government holdings.

Official city, county, and state government sites. Compile your city, county, and state websites in an online guide or library blog, or print out a list of resources that can be placed at the reference desk. Make it easy for library staff to find and use these resources, and update them as needed. Also include links to other local and state libraries. Having knowledgeable staff available is a big help if your library is located in an area where patrons have limited internet access and must use the library's computers to download forms and get information.

City-Data.com, www.city-data.com, is a great resource for overall area research, especially for people looking for information on relocating to or from a particular area and for those looking at starting businesses. Developed originally as a tool for real estate agents, it has in-depth information on large and small cities in every state. The information and statistics come from a variety of sources, most of which are not cited specifically by City-Data. However, the information is trustworthy, and the site is updated frequently.

Social Explorer, www.socialexplorer.com, is a subscription-based database that is an excellent resource for every library. *Social Explorer* contains retrospective and current information from the US Census (1790-2010), the American Community Survey (ACS), and other agencies. This is a very helpful site for anyone wanting to research demographic information on local, state, and national levels, and it is a great place to direct patrons who are planning business ventures. Users can search either by using maps or reports and can build their own datasets. This site also works well with GIS-related projects. There are helpful videos and other tools to help you and your users work with this site.

*ReferenceUSA,* www.referenceusa.com, is an essential resource for finding business and residential information. It is especially helpful for those looking into the types of businesses in specific zip code areas. If your library does not have this database, check with other libraries in your area to see if one of them subscribes to it.

Rich Blocks Poor Blocks, www.richblockspoorblocks.com, is a map of income and rent in every neighborhood in the United States. All data comes from the most current ACS. It is another good resource for those doing business-related research.

# FEDERAL AGENCY RESOURCES

## *General*

USA.gov, www.usa.gov, the "one-stop shopping" gateway to US federal government agency websites and the wealth of information and services they contain. A number of these links are highlighted in the following sections. Users can also check the FAQ link to find answers to common queries, and they can also contact government agencies, Congress, and the Executive Branch through this site. It is also available in Spanish, GobiernoUSA.gov, https://gobierno.usa.gov.

Google, www.google.com. When I first started as a librarian, Google Uncle Sam was *the* online resource most recommended to me by other librarians. In 2011 Google discontinued its Uncle Sam Search, but all the resources are still available through the main Google search box. Search engines such as Google are helpful because they give you a starting point for finding relevant information. Here is a tip: If you use site:.gov and your search term(s), all your results will be .gov resources only (e.g., *site:.gov affordable care*). Starting your search with Google can be easier for finding the titles and numbers of specific hearings or Congressional sessions. You can then go back to the official government search engines, such as FDsys or Congress.gov, to find the full-text documents. Bing and other search engines are also very helpful.

FDsys, www.gpo.gov/fdsys, provides free online access to official publications from all three branches of the federal government. Users can search for, browse, and download authenticated PDFs of government publications. Authentication means that the original documents have not been altered in any way before they were uploaded by the GPO. These documents also contain digital signatures. You can see all the collections and related resources by clicking on Browse Government Publications. FDsys also allows researchers to search through all the relevant collections using its simple search box. Note: FDsys will be replaced by govinfo.gov, which is currently in beta.

MetaLib, http://metalib.gpo.gov. This tool provides a federated search interface across a wide range of federal agency databases, while FDsys provides authentic official documents from the three branches of government.

**Congress.gov,** www.congress.gov. This Library of Congress site contains legislative histories, the legislative process, bill tracking, and background information on Congressional members, lobbyists, organizations, and funding. (This site has superseded THOMAS.gov.)

**Census.gov,** www.census.gov, is an invaluable resource for general and academic users wanting to find in-depth demographic information. There are a number of interactive internet data tools, such as the County Business and Demographics Map, available. The Census' information portal is American Fact Finder where you will find decennial census information dating back to 1790, the most current ACS statistics, and additional statistical series. Databases such as *Social Explorer* and *ReferenceUSA* are also good resources to direct users to data based on census reports.

### Business

**BusinessUSA,** http://business.usa.gov. This site has all kinds of information related to business planning, including starting a business, hiring, veteran's assistance, access to financing, and much more. Users can enter their zip codes to find offices and resources close to them if they need face-to-face assistance.

**US Bureau of Labor Statistics,** www.bls.gov, from the US Department of Labor. Users can access this site to do research on employment trends and opportunities and find information on other workplace topics. The full-text version of the *Occupational Outlook Handbook* is accessible through this site.

**IRS.gov,** www.irs.gov. Find tax forms and instruction booklets for individuals and businesses, information on how to file, and FAQs. If you are in charge of tax forms and tax information at your library, highlight this site at tax time and make sure library staff knows about it. If your library also provides printed tax forms and instruction booklets, you will be contacted by the IRS distribution center well in advance of tax time to get the items you need.

**US Small Business Administration,** www.sba.gov. This site is essential for users exploring starting and managing small businesses. It includes tools for creating business plans, getting local assistance for loans and grants, and qualifying for government assistance.

## Geographic Information Systems (GIS) resources

If you are new to GIS or are already well-versed in using data to build GIS maps, these resources will provide you all kinds of data sets. A few are listed here to get you started, and there are many more free and commercial sites to choose from.

**Data.gov,** www.data.gov, contains over 100,000 datasets from federal government agencies and sub-agencies.

**Stanford Geospatial Center,** https://library.stanford.edu/research/stanford-geospatial-center/data, links to freely available local, state, and global datasets.

**ESRI's ArcGIS,** www.arcgis.com. Many academic and public libraries are adding this software to their computers. ArcGIS is featured in the book *Getting Started with GIS: A LITA Guide* and its companion website www.neal-schuman.com/gis.

**Google Earth,** www.google.com/earth, and Google Earth Pro have tools for building GIS-enhanced maps, including a variety of layers.

## Medical

**MedLinePlus,** https://medlineplus.gov, from the National Library of Medicine. A very comprehensive and user-friendly website with information on every health topic imaginable. It includes a medical dictionary, health advice for all age groups, and videos and tutorials. Some, but not all, links have information in Spanish, Vietnamese, Arabic, Chinese, and other languages.

**Centers for Disease Control and Prevention (CDC),** www.cdc.gov, covers many health and safety topics, including epidemics in the United States and worldwide, environmental health, healthy living, data and statistics, and more. If patrons are concerned about medical issues such as flu season and where and how to get vaccinations, this is the place to direct them.

## Statistical

Many government agencies have statistical information, but here are a few general and specific resources.

**American FactFinder,** http://factfinder.census.gov/faces/nav/jsf/pages/index.xhtml, from the US Census. Comprehensive data on all fifty states and territories gathered from the Census, the ACS, and other official statistical surveys. This is an easy to understand site and is especially useful for students doing state research.

**FedStats,** www.fedstats.gov, is a collection of statistics from more than a hundred agencies. The A-Z links are very comprehensive.

**Bureau of Labor Statistics,** www.bls.gov/eag/eag.us.htm. Find state and national statistics on employment, unemployment, productivity, pricing, and more. Also connect to the *Occupational Outlook Handbook*, www.bls.gov/ooh/home.htm.

**National Criminal Justice Reference Center (NCJRS),** www.ncjrs.gov. This resource has a very comprehensive topical index including justice and drug-related information, crime statistics, campus safety guidelines, and additional information relating to crime.

**United Nations (UN) Statistical Data,** http://unstats.un.org/unsd/data bases.htm. Users can search for and download statistical resources in the UN system. The site is also a good resource for doing country research.

### Travel and Country Research

*Travel.state.gov,* http://travel.state.gov, from the US Department of State. Users can plan for trips by finding out how to apply for and renew passports, check travel warnings and alerts, find US consulates, and get other travel-related and country-specific information.

*World Factbook,* https://www.cia.gov/library/publications/resources/the -world-factbook/index.html, from the CIA. Comprehensive demographic, economic, political, and historical information on 267 world entities. An excellent site for students, travelers, researchers, and anyone else needing country information.

### Weather and Geography

National Oceanic and Atmospheric Administration (NOAA), www.noaa .gov. Comprehensive information about weather and weather-related topics. This is an especially useful site for tracking and updating severe weather events. The National Weather Service is also working on a GIS data portal, www.nws.noaa.gov/gis.

US Geological Survey (USGS), www.usgs.gov. This site has thousands of downloadable topographic maps, including historical maps. Having a scanner and printer designated especially for this site are great for researchers. Also, the maps on this site work well with GIS software.

## FEDERAL LEGISLATIVE RESOURCES

**GovTrack.us,** www.govtrack.us, lets users find summaries and full-text of pending legislation in state legislatures and in Congress, as well as the funding, voting records, and ideology of Congress members. For users needing to find full-text of bills, the links will take them to Congress.gov. A very clear and easy site to understand.

**C-SPAN,** www.c-span.org. Users can follow live Congressional hearings, news conferences, conference proceedings, and other Congressional-related topics. C-SPAN is an excellent resource for students and researchers and contains archives of older hearings and interviews.

**Sunlight Foundation,** http://sunlightfoundation.com. The Sunlight Foundation is a national, non-partisan, and non-profit organization that uses reports and statistics from the Federal government to make charts, graphs, and reports that explain how the government works, focusing on the role of money and influence in politics. The information is user-friendly and easy to understand. Representatives from the Sunlight Foundation often give presentations at FDLP meetings.

**The Federal Register Tutorial,** www.archives.gov/federal-register/tutorial, from the National Archives. Explains what the *Federal Register* (FR) and the *Code of Federal Regulations* (CFR) are, what they contain, and how researchers can use them, especially for legal research.

## HISTORICAL AND GENEALOGICAL RESOURCES

**American Memory,** http://memory.loc.gov, is a site full of treasures, such as A Century of Lawmaking for a New Nation, which includes the *American State Papers*, the *Serial Set, Statutes at Large 1789–1875*, and more. There are many unique collections, originating from the Library of Congress, available at this site, including a lot of ephemera (signs, posters, brochures, etc.). A very good source for genealogical research.

**The National Archives and Records Administration** (NARA), www.archives.gov, is a great source for genealogists and historians. While many of their resources are not available in full-text online, users can find online research tools and contact NARA to make appointments to view records at the NARA headquarters in Washington, DC.

**Internet Archive,** http://archive.org, contains an ever-expanding digital library of resources. Government-specific subjects include historic and current government hearings, pamphlets, training films, news reports, music, and other archives. Access is free. This is one of my favorite sites.

**Founders Online,** http://founders.archives.gov, is a partnership between the National Archives and the University of Virginia Press that makes the full-text of historical documents of the major founders of the United States available online. Included are documents of George Washington, Thomas Jefferson, James Madison, Benjamin Franklin, Alexander Hamilton, and John Adams (and family). A great resource for American history buffs.

**US Citizenship and Immigration Services (USCIS),** www.uscis.gov/HGWebinars. This site leads users to history and genealogy webinars, including schedules for upcoming webinars. Users can also learn how to get help with family research through USCIS.

**The HathiTrust Digital Library,** www.hathitrust.org, offers users millions of titles from academic and research institutions around the world. Many are available in full-text, while others are not available online due to copyright restrictions. Digitized federal US government documents have been included from a number of university collections. Many research libraries are partners in the HathiTrust, so check to see if yours is participating.

## LEGAL RESEARCH

Patrons may ask for legal help in person or online. While you cannot give out any legal advice, you can lead your patrons to reliable and useful resources. Also, find and keep a list of law libraries in your area that are accessible to the public and refer your users to them. Get to know the law librarians in your area. Cities and counties usually have law libraries, as do universities with law schools.

**FindLaw,** www.findlaw.com, provides information on a variety of legal topics, lawyer profiles, answers to legal questions, and more. Users can also purchase forms.

Georgetown University's Free and Low Cost Legal Research Guide, www.law.georgetown.edu/library/research/guides/freelowcost.cfm, contains guides, tutorials, citation information, and more.

*Public Library of Law,* www.plol.org. Users can access cases back to 1997 from the US Supreme Court and the Courts of Appeals in all fifty states. They can also research US federal statutory law and codes from all fifty states. The site also links to regulations, court rules, constitutions, and downloadable legal forms.

*Statutes at Large,* www.constitution.org/uslaw/sal/sal.htm. This is the complete and easily searchable digitized set starting with Volume 1, 1789-99 and going through Volume 129, 2015. A very good site for legal researchers and historians.

## INTERNATIONAL ORGANIZATIONS AND RESOURCES

Below are links to well-known international organizations and related resources. Many publications can be downloaded or ordered directly from these sites, and most IGOs and NGOs have reports and statistics that can be accessed through their own websites.

European Union (EU) Law and Publications
   http://publications.europa.eu

International Monetary Fund (IMF)
   www.imf.org/external/publications/index.htm

North Atlantic Treaty Organization (NATO) Library
   http://www.nato.int/cps/en/natohq/publications.htm

Organization for Economic Cooperation and Development (OECD) Bookshop
   www.oecdbookshop.org/oecd/index.asp?lang=EN

United Nations (UN) Publications
   https://shop.un.org

World Bank Publications
   www.worldbank.org/en/publication/reference

## RELATED RESOURCES

The LibGuides Community site has many guides featuring international publications and websites, http://community.libguides.com.

**GODORT's International Documents Task Force (IDTF)**, http://wikis.ala.org/godort/index.php/International_Documents, contains a lot of information and a list of competencies for librarians handling international documents.

**ALA's INTL-DOC** discussion group, www.ala.org/godort/taskforces/internationaldocuments/intldoc, is for librarians who deal with resources and information pertaining to international documents from government sources and IGOs and NGOs.

**GODORT's Toolbox for Processing and Cataloging International Government Documents**, http://wikis.ala.org/godort/index.php/Toolbox_for_Processing_and_Cataloging_International_Govern ment_Documents, *explains collection management of international documents and provides links to many helpful sites.*

**Online international newspapers** are available through websites and subscription databases such as ProQuest, Readex, EBSCO, and others. Two good free sources for current US and world newspapers, in English and other languages, are ThePaperboy.com, www.thepaperboy.com, and Onlinenewspapers.com, www.onlinenewspapers.com.

## PUBLISHERS OF INTERNATIONAL AND GOVERNMENT INFORMATION

**Bernan**, www.bernan.com, publishes reports from many international agencies including the United Nations, UNESCO, the World Trade Organization, OECD, and the World Bank. They also publish US government publications, including ProQuest's print version of the *Statistical Abstract of the United States.*

**Renouf Books**, www.renoufbooks.com, publishes international and domestic agency reports, labor and trade overviews, economic surveys, and more. Bernan and Renouf jointly publish and distribute some agency reports.

Many libraries use collection management tools such as YBP (Yankee Book Peddler) and its GOBI[3] ordering system. With these systems, a collection profile can be set up for automatic viewing or ordering of the latest publications from these publishers.

# REFERENCE BOOK PUBLISHERS

ALCTS, ABC-CLIO, Europa Press, Gale, Greenwood Press, Libraries Unlimited, and SAGE (distributor for CQ Press) publish excellent reference books and offer online resources for US government and international organization documents.

# DATABASES

Congressional Quarterly (CQ) databases, available via subscription or purchase from CQ Press, feature reports, statistics, and opposing viewpoints sections that are easy to understand and very useful to researchers, especially students working on position papers.

- *CQ Global Researcher* contains reports on key global issues.
- *CQ Public Affairs Collection* includes reports on twenty-two specific public affairs areas.
- *CQ Researcher Plus Archive* contains reports spanning 1923 to the present. Researchers can follow the coverage of issues over time.
- *CQ Voting and Elections Collection* includes reports, election data, and other information related to US elections.

The HathiTrust Digital Library has a large number of full-text government documents. This is a terrific starting place for finding obscure documents. The only drawback is that SuDoc numbers are not included in the metadata, so searching can be difficult if you don't know the agencies that generated the documents.

*LexisNexis Academic* lets users search for US and international law information and legal cases. It also has US and world news and company information.

ProQuest's databases are very good places to find reports, statistics, and other primary sources. If your library does not currently subscribe to these databases, see if other libraries in your area provide access.

- ProQuest *Congressional* contains Congressional publications, information about members of Congress, historical documents, and more resources related to the Congress.
- ProQuest *Statistical Insight* includes statistical information gathered from a number of US government and global

agencies. Users can compile and download their own data sets.

- *Statistical Abstract of the United States.* This comprehensive resource, originating from the US Census Bureau, ceased publication in 2011. However, ProQuest stepped in to continue it and it is now available commercially as an ongoing serial publication through Bernan and online through ProQuest.

## GENERAL SEARCH ENGINES

**Google and Google Search, Yahoo, and Bing** are excellent resources for finding reports, statistics, polling, and other government-related information. Always check sites to see when they were last updated and research the organizations that sponsor them.

### Recommended Reading

Dodsworth, Eva. 2012. *Getting Started with GIS: A LITA Guide.* New York, NY: Neal-Schuman Publishers, Inc.

**five**

# Issues, Challenges, and Opportunities

Many studies and reports have been commissioned and issued in recent years by the GPO and the FDLP to help them identify ways to operate more effectively. There have been positive and negative responses from the government information community to these reports, and as Keiser says, "Through the past 20 years, depository librarians have participated in numerous studies, providing their comments and ideas as to how the program might evolve; now, they are ripe for action, not additional research efforts" (Keiser, 2011). Many depository librarians are frustrated that there is no clear road forward. Since ninety-seven percent of content issued by the GPO is born digital, many FDLP librarians and their library administrators are asking why they are still in the program when so much is available online, not just from the GPO, but also from resources previously mentioned in this guide—agency websites, government-related agencies, Google, the Internet Archive, et al.

Have FDLs become redundant, just warehousing underutilized print collections? Depository librarians, the GPO, and FDLP are still working on ideas for effective innovation, relevance, and outreach, but some see the GPO and FDLP as obsolete and are calling for the end to both (Seavey, 2010). Two comprehensive reports were commissioned by the GPO and

FDLP to address this and other issues: The National Academy of Public Administration (NAPA)'s *Rebooting the Government Printing Office: Keeping America Informed in the Digital Age* and Ithaka S+R's *Modeling a Sustainable Future for the United States Federal Depository Program's Network of Libraries in the 21st Century: Final Report of Ithaka S+R to the Government Printing Office*. While it had been reviewed and discussed in depth by depository librarians and other stakeholders, the final report from the Ithaka study was rejected by the GPO in 2011. In her statement, Mary Alice Baish, the current Superintendent of Documents, said:

> In response to a 2009 recommendation by the Depository Library Council to the Public Printer, the US Government Printing Office (GPO) contracted with Ithaka S+R (Ithaka) in September 2010 to develop practical and sustainable models for the Federal Depository Library Program (FDLP). After a very comprehensive analysis by GPO, the final report prepared by Ithaka was deemed unacceptable under the terms of the contract. The models proposed by Ithaka are not practical and sustainable to meet the mission, goals, and principles of the FDLP (Baish, 2011).

Considering that Ithaka continually updated the GPO and the DLC on its findings during the process of preparing the report, this was a disappointing response from the GPO. Some criticisms of the report also came from the depository librarian community, including comments that the report was too narrow in focus, addressed issues mainly related to print resources, and did not take into account "the needs of ultimate users—the American public" (Keiser, 2011). The NAPA study has also garnered criticism, especially for one of its suggestions that taxpayers be charged to access FDsys. Since taxpayers have already paid for these resources, charging double is seen as an unlikely solution to the problem of budget shortfalls at the GPO (McGilvray, 2013).

## ISSUES AND CHALLENGES

The role of the GPO as the main distributor of print and online information is challenged by government agencies that directly upload information to their own websites. This bypasses the GPO, its cataloging records, the PURL system, and the authentication process. When individual librarians find out about these documents they often post the links to national and state government documents discussion groups, such as GOVDOC-L, so that they can be downloaded and cataloged in local library catalogs or be posted to online research guides and blogs. However, because not all librarians subscribe to the same discussion groups, and others may not have permission to upload individual resources, this is a haphazard method. A lot of potentially useful information continues to slip through the cracks because there is no official overall harvesting program in place.

Many of the provisions in the US Code of Federal Regulations Title 44, (chapters 1901-1916): Library Depository Program need to be overhauled as they still mainly address the GPO's distribution of printed materials, not the management, control, and coordination of electronic resources. Revised regulations also need to address how the GPO can work with federal and other outside agencies to handle "fugitive" documents—reports and other documents posted by individual agencies to their own websites. The links to these documents are often temporary, so they disappear completely or the URLs change, making them difficult to retrieve at a later date. Having these documents harvested by the GPO assures that the links are secure and authenticated.

Recent legislation passed in 2014, 44 USCS § 4101: Access to Federal Electronic Information, mandates that the Superintendent of Documents, under the direction of the Public Printer, shall maintain an electronic directory of federal electronic information and provide access to the *Congressional Record*, the *Federal Register*, and other appropriate document through the directory. PL 107–347, the E-Government Act of 2002, established an Office of Electronic Government within the Office of Management & Budget (OMB), to coordinate, implement, and facilitate interagency e-government projects; to address issues related to fugitive documents; and clarify the role of the GPO in working with agencies and departments to better coordinate and authenticate digital resources. While these are good efforts, most chapters of Title 44 Chapter 19 need to be updated entirely to reflect current realities, but it does not appear that Congress feels it is a pressing priority. The last major overhaul was done in 1962—over fifty years ago!

The Association of Research Libraries (ARL) and other academic organizations are looking at establishing more flexible working models for FDLP libraries. The 2009 report, *White Paper: Strategic Directions for the Federal Depository Library Program*, outlined a number of key elements to a new service model for FDLs, including these suggestions: networked-based collaboration between GPO and FDLs and among the depository libraries; formation of new partnerships among FDLs; regional preservation of specific print and electronic collections; and more flexibility for collaboration among FDLs (Association of Research Libraries, 2009). Because FDLs now get many of their resources electronically, the focus should be less on collection development and more on harnessing the expertise of government information professionals to address the use, preservation, access, and overall marketing of these collections.

A 2011 budget-cutting initiative from the OMB required the federal government to cut its 24,000 websites in half by mid-2012 for an estimated savings of $10 million a year. This was seen as an opportunity to remove "redundant, out-dated, or hard to use" sites (Opam, 2011). The University of North Texas (UNT), through its CyberCemetery project and website, http://govinfo.library.unt.edu, has been working on archiving a number of government websites that are no longer available. The FDLP's Content Partnerships Program is also working with UNT and other libraries to ensure that the public has permanent access to older electronic information. Users can also find links to obsolete agency websites and other links by searching with the Internet Archive Wayback Machine.

At the state and local level, many academic libraries are relocating parts of their print collections, including government documents, to more obscure and perhaps less accessible parts of their libraries, or to off-site storage, in order to free up space for expanded computer and technology centers, such as Learning Commons spaces. Space for government documents in particular is being scrutinized by library administrators because of their perceived lack of use by general users and researchers (Johnson, 2012), and the perception that most content is now available online. While it is true that many of the essential titles, such as the *Congressional Record* and the *Federal Register*, have been digitized and are available in databases or on websites, much of the older content, especially prior to the 1990s, is not yet readily available electronically. Many researchers must still use print versions of House and Senate hearings, the *Congressional Record* and its indexes. The database *Hein Online* does have deep digital archives of government documents, but it is a subscription database mainly used in law libraries, and access will be lost if libraries cease their subscriptions.

Although the FDLP requires that their logo appear on entrance doors and the library website home page, some libraries choose not to advertise themselves as FDLs, either physically or online. Many patrons may not be aware that their local libraries have a government information collection as well as experienced personnel to help them with research.

Outdated equipment also hampers access to government information. The GPO has issued much of its content on microfiche from the 1970s to the present, but many libraries have not updated their equipment, resulting in having inoperable or no available microfiche readers and printers. There is also the issue of older CD-ROMs not operating on upgraded computers, leading libraries to weed their CD-ROM collections, or simply discarding them entirely even if the content has not been superseded by electronic versions. These equipment problems can put many FDLs out of compliance with legal requirements as specified in the *Legal Requirements & Program Regulations of the FDLP, Physical Facilities and Maintenance of the Collection*, items 22 and 23. While it is the responsibility of FDLP libraries to provide updated computers and printers, the GPO does not provide funding for these upgrades.

Funding shortfalls negatively affect future plans for updating and expanding FDsys and additional services provided by the GPO, Library of Congress, and other government agencies. The House and Senate omnibus funding bill passed in December 2011 gave the GPO $90.7 million for fiscal 2012, down from 2011's $135 million. The White House budget request for 2012 was $148 million (Jacobs, 2011), and the GPO's fiscal year 2014 budget request was $128.5 million (Brudnick, 2013). Across-the-board budget cuts (sequestration), enacted by the Budget Control Act of 2011, began on March 1, 2013 and have caused many federal agency employees, including those at the GPO, to go on furlough or take early retirement. The Library of Congress has cut down on the number of reading rooms in its Washington, DC, headquarters and has cut staff. The GPO is leasing some space in its Washington, DC, plant to other federal agencies and private companies. Many states and municipalities are also facing similar cutbacks in print and electronic government information dissemination. For example, in 2011 the Texas State Library and Archives Commission had about two-thirds of its operating budget cut, causing the elimination of staff and severely curtailing distribution of tangible copies of materials to regional and selective depositories in the state (Walters, 2013). The Texas State Librarian currently has very little staff to help with the needs of repositories and selectives in Texas, especially for overseeing weeding procedures.

Decreases in funding for statistics-gathering agencies, such as the Census and the ACS, are especially worrisome because these resources are used by many public and private organizations for critical decision-making and ongoing planning. The kinds of questions the Census and the ACS can ask are also under scrutiny, and both are vulnerable to the shifting political winds in Congress and the Executive Branch (Rampell, 2012). However, some for-profit database providers and publishers are stepping in to support and add enhancements to resources that have lost funding. For example, the *Statistical Abstract*, published until 2012 through the Department of Commerce and the Census, is being handled by ProQuest and is now known as the *ProQuest Statistical Abstract of the United States*. This is good news for libraries that can afford to buy this database or get a subscription to the print version distributed by Bernan, but access has been cut off for many patrons and businesses that do not have the budget for it.

The cost of printing and distributing the *Federal Register*, the *Congressional Record*, and other essential titles is being scrutinized by Congress and the Executive Branch due to the ease of putting digital versions online. While many government documents librarians advocate for the continued printing of these resources, digital resources are the most used by the public. To avoid loss of access, government information librarians are recommending that multiple copies of essential documents be digitized and available from a variety of websites, both government and commercial. This program is called LOCKSS-USDOCS (Lots of Copies Keep Stuff Safe). Libraries are looking at the content of their documents collections, especially older items, to see if it is worth digitizing them.

Many documents librarians in public, academic, law, and special libraries are no longer assigned only to government collections, with management of government information accounting for a small part of one's overall job. Therefore, librarians must try to build time into their schedules to deal with ongoing government information collection and management issues. In my library I also serve as the history and political science librarian, and while these subjects dovetail neatly with government documents, I cannot devote as much time to collection management as I would like, especially for much-needed weeding projects. Also, support staff to do the processing of documents and downloading of cataloging records has been cut or eliminated in many libraries.

It is also noteworthy that, as of 2014, the Canadian counterpart to the FDLP, the Depository Services Program (DSP), has ceased to exist with the explanation being that all federal documents are now online so there is no need for a distribution program.

> The DSP kept track of the publication of government documents. Now each library will have to chase after every document, and then make individual arrangements to obtain it. As each library makes its own decisions, we will see a patchwork of partial coverage emerge, with each library collecting according to local needs and budgets (Kaufman and Moon, 2013).

Many Canadian libraries with documents collections are also no longer restrained by DSP guidelines regarding weeding and are free to completely discard these collections. While the US Public Printer is looking into a new national plan for the future of the FDLP, it could meet the same fate as the DSP.

## OPPORTUNITIES

Even with all the challenges facing government information librarians now and in the future, there are still many ways you can promote your collections. Patrons and researchers especially want historical and genealogical information, and there are several great websites and mobile apps that deal with healthcare, education, travel, and other needs of US citizens. Through outreach, you can market these resources and become known as an expert in your field. Here are some of the ways you can market your collections.

### Create an Online Presence

Utilizing inexpensive or free software will help you offer fun and innovative ways to introduce your users to government information resources.

LibGuides (Springshare). Many public and academic libraries use this software to create inviting and informative websites for all kinds of subject areas and special research needs. You can upload and annotate resources so that users can access relevant sites easily. Links to videos, maps, blogs, and social media can also be added to your site. Stuck for ideas? The LibGuides Community site, http://libguides.com/community, connects you to government documents and information from libraries in the United States and around the world. Make sure you do not put too much information on these pages and check your links regularly to make sure they still work.

**Other online guide software.** If your library cannot support LibGuides, try sites that offer free software, such as SubjectsPlus, www.subjectsplus.com, or LibData, www.libdata.com. Check with your web services department to get permission to download software and see if they can help you build and maintain your guides.

**Webinars** are a great way to reach out to other librarians and specific user groups. For example, webinars targeted to genealogy buffs can focus on how to search and use American Memory's *Serial Set* and the *American State Papers*, the Census, or government-related resources like *Social Explorer*. Showing users how to access the features and links in general sites such as USA.gov, MedlinePlus, and the CDC can be invaluable. Webinars can be conducted through your organization's webinar software or by partnering with other organizations. I recently did a webinar, *I Didn't Know I Could Do That!*, for ALA members as part of GODORT's Education Committee. It featured several government websites and alternative sites that could be used during a government shutdown. I learned from feedback that many librarians do not know about the many government and government-related online resources that are available.

**Blogs** can be a great way to highlight resources and also invite comments from your users. I recommend creating free blogs with Blogger, http://blogger.com, or WordPress, http://wordpress.org. Images, videos, and links can easily be added. Be sure to update them regularly to keep your blog(s) relevant.

**Social Media,** such as Facebook, www.facebook.com, Twitter, http://twitter.com, and LinkedIn, www.linkedin.com, are good places to post information and links. You can have fun posting links to websites, news, mobile apps, images, and other resources. Use software like HootSuite, http://hootsuite.com, to connect all your social media accounts and check your usage stats. Facebook and Twitter especially allow you to distribute news and resources quickly to staff and the public. Check with your library administration on any policies set up to govern the use of social media. There may be restrictions in place monitoring what kinds of information can be disseminated under an organization's name and logo.

### Instruction Classes

Government resources can be incorporated into all kinds of classroom instruction and activities, from public schools to university settings. Many government resources cover the humanities, social sciences, and sciences and can also be used to help with grant searches and other avenues for funding. Public libraries also offer classes on genealogy, small business development, and other areas of interest to the community. If you teach from your LibGuides or use similar software it is easy to include links to government information databases, websites, and resources such as training videos. It is also a good way to keep usage statistics on these resources and boost traffic to often overlooked resources.

For basic history and political science instruction sessions, I recommend the following:

American Memory, the Census, Congress.gov, NARA, CIA *World Factbook*, MedLine Plus, USA.gov, Bureau of Labor Statistics, Statistical Abstract of the United States, Data.gov, and *Social Explorer. Ben's Guide to U.S. Government for Kids* is a wonderful place for K–12 students to find information and basic historic documents, such as the Declaration of Independence.

These related databases and websites also incorporate government information:

*Historical Statistics of the United States* from Gale, ProQuest *Congressional*, ProQuest *Statistical Insight*, Google Patents, and GovTrack.us.

For graduate students and faculty, I use more specific government and non-governmental sites depending on the subject area:

The Supreme Court of the United States, the *Federal Register*, the *Congressional Record*, *The United States Statutes at Large*, HathiTrust, Law Library of Congress, FedStats, and Public Library of Law. The Internet Archive is especially useful for finding streaming videos of hearings and other archival government-related material.

Congressional Quarterly (CQ Press) collections have both print and online resources that incorporate government information. See all the collections at the CQ Press Library site, http://library.cqpress.com.

Campus law libraries are likely to have databases and resources like *Westlaw*, *Hein Online*, and *LexisNexis* for legal information you may not have access to at your main library. Law librarians can also work with you to find resources and offer research help to students and faculty.

### Promotional activities

Promoting your government resources to coincide with elections, tax season, and state or federal holidays such as Independence Day, Constitution Day, and Thanksgiving can connect users in a meaningful way with your library, physically and virtually. I make sure to have printed forms and instruction booklets ready during tax time, and I also highlight the IRS website on the library's home page and my government information online guide. For local, state, and national elections links to voter information and issues are very helpful. Try to include websites that are politically neutral, such as the League of Women Voters.

Check your print collection to see if there are informative, fun, and unique things in which the public may be interested in (e.g., old cookbooks, posters, historical reports, etc.). You can mount displays and invite the public to view them and also create companion online guides to go with them.

You may be a designated depository for specific and unique resources, for example, documents related to a Superfund clean-up site in your area. Let your patrons know these resources are available and put them in a place that is easily accessible.

On-campus and community organizations, such as those for veterans or people with disabilities, would welcome your expertise in helping users connect to unknown resources, like the Department of Veterans Affairs, at the local and national level. Post timely information on these resources to your blog, the library's home page, your social networking sites, and any other outlet that might be seen by your target audience.

FDLP outreach resources, www.fdlp.gov/outreach, provide a variety of free promotional items such as posters, buttons, table tents, flyers, and bookmarks. If you want to plan a government-related event in your library or community, you can go solo or partner with other FDLs in your city or state. If your FDL is hitting a milestone, like a twenty-fifth anniversary, invite the public to celebrate and have a display of your resources.

Finding ways to use government information is fun and creative! The more you learn about these resources, the more you will want to spread the word to others. After having worked with government information in my library now for several years, I have really come to appreciate and love these materials.

## References

Association of Research Libraries. 2009. *White Paper: Strategic Directions for the Federal Depository Library Program*. www.arl.org/storage/documents/publications/fdlp-strategic-directions-april09.pdf.

Baish, Mary Alice. 2011. Statement from the U.S. Government Printing Office. www.uflib.ufl.edu/docs/ithaka-final-report-and-gpo-statement.pdf.

Brudnick, Ida A. 2013. Legislative Branch: FY2014 Appropriations. p. 17. https://archive.org/details/R43151LegislativeBranchFY2014Appropriations-crs.

Jacobs, James A. "Privatization of GPO, Defunding of FDsys and the Future of the FDLP". *Free Government Information*, August 11, 2011. http://freegovinfo.info/node/3416.

Johnson, Bernadette. 2012. "Government Document Usage and Awareness in Higher Education." *DttP: Documents to the People* 4, no. 3: 22. http://wikis.ala.org/godort/images/b/b4/DttP40n3.pdf.

Kaufman, Amy, and Jeff Moon. "Farewell to a Building Block of Democracy." OttawaCitizen.com, November 4, 2013. http://www.pressreader.com/canada/ottawa-citizen/20131104/281741267175705.

Keiser, Barbie E. "GPO Disapproves of Report on the Future of Federal Depository Libraries." *Information Today*, August 25, 2011. http://newsbreaks.infotoday.com/NewsBreaks/GPO-Disapproves-of-Report-on-the-Future-of-Federal-Depository-Libraries-77289.asp.

McGilvray, Jessica. "New GPO Report Suggests Charging Taxpayers Twice for Government Information." *District Dispatch*, February 12, 2013. www.districtdispatch.org/2013/02/new-gpo-report-suggests-charging-taxpayers-twice-for-government-info.

Opam, Kwame. "U.S. Government Shutting Down Half Its Websites." Gizmodo, June 15, 2011. http://gizmodo.com/5812115/us-government-shutting-down-half-its-websites.

Rampell, Catherine. "The Beginning of the End of the Census?" *New York Times Sunday Review*, May 19, 2012. www.nytimes.com/2012/05/20/sunday-review/the-debate-over-the-american-community-survey.html?module=Search&mabReward=relbias%3Ar&_r=0.

Seavey, Charles A. 2010. "GPO Must Go: The Government Printing Office is an Obsolete Relic." *American Libraries* 41, no. 10: 33. http://freegovinfo.info/files/Seavey-gpo-must-go.pdf.

Walters, Edgar. "Texas Libraries Face Federal Funding Cuts." *The Texas Tribune*, November 7, 2013. www.texastribune.org/2013/11/07/texas-libraries-face-federal-funding-cuts.

## Recommended Reading

Federal Depository Library Program. 2011. Collection Maintenance. www.gpo.gov/libraries.

Housewright, Ross, and Roger C. Schonfeld. 2011. *Modeling a Sustainable Future for the United States Federal Depository Program's Network of Libraries in the 21st Century: Final Report of Ithaka S+R to the Government Printing Office.* www.uflib.ufl.edu/docs/ithaka-final-report-and-gpo-statement.pdf.

Keiser, Barbie E. "End User Survey of Federal Depository Libraries." *Information Today*, September 26, 2011. http://newsbreaks.infotoday.com/NewsBreaks/End-User-Survey-of-Federal-Depository-Libraries-77897.asp.

National Academy of Public Administration. 2013. *Rebooting the Government Printing Office: Keeping America Informed in the Digital Age.* (Advisory No. 2170). Washington, DC: National Academy of Public Administration. www.napawash.org/wp-content/uploads/2013/02/GPO-Final.pdf.

# ABOUT THE AUTHOR

**ALEXANDRA SIMONS** has worked in academic libraries since 2007, specializing in instruction, reference, and collection development. After serving as a reference librarian at the Art Institute of Houston library, she moved to the M.D. Anderson Library at the University of Houston. She currently serves as the subject librarian for history, political science, and government information. Alexandra actively participates in the Government Documents Round Table (GODORT) with the Texas Library Association and the American Library Association. She is also a member of the American Historical Association.

CPSIA information can be obtained
at www.ICGtesting.com
Printed in the USA
FFOW02n1144300417
35021FF